An Introduc

AN INTRODUCTION TO
Media Relations
FOR NONPROFIT ORGANIZATIONS

MARIA SATIRA

Maria Satira
P. O. Box 2852
Greenville, North Carolina 27836
maria@mariasatira.com
www.mariasatira.com

Printed in the United States of America
First Printing, 2021

ISBN: 978-0-578-96647-2

Editor & Consultant
Lita P. Ward, the Editorial Midwife LPW
Editing & Consulting Services, LLC
lpwediting@gmail.com
www.litapward.com

Cover Design
Mike Satira
mike@mikesatira.com
www.mikesatira.com

For my husband:

Thank you for supporting the charitable causes that are important to our family. Because of you, our community is a better place.

Table of Contents

INTRODUCTION

One of this book's specific goals is to teach your organization several effective methods to obtain the positive media attention it deserves. Within our great nation, there are an estimated 12.3 million staff members[1] and more than 63 million volunteers[2] in the nonprofit sector. Your work is important, appreciated, and admirable. Because you and your organization are making a difference in your community, I aspire to help you increase your visibility.

As a news media, marketing, and communications professional throughout the past decade, I've been

---

[1] Bureau of Labor Statistics, U.S. Department of Labor, The Economics Daily

[2] Bureau of Labor Statistics, U.S. Department of Labor, Economic News Release

exposed to the incredible work of various not-for-profits. These experiences include national, local, and grassroots organizations. I've served as a board member, committee representative, and volunteer for several of them. These personal and unique experiences taught me the value and importance of developing an effective communication strategy when working with news and media outlets.

This guide features various topics and situations within media relations, regardless of budget, location, or staff size. In addition, the end of each chapter includes a 'TIDBIT' which features more details, personal stories, and creative ideas to further support your organization's media relations efforts. You will discover many helpful techniques, such as the **STRONG** method, to communicate and control the messaging of your mission. The contents of this book will be beneficial to you and your organization as you look to enhance or strengthen your media relations strategy.

1

UNDERSTANDING THE POWER OF WORDS

Words are powerful.

If you take away anything from this book, I sincerely hope that you revisit these three words daily, "Words are powerful!" As defined by Merriam-Webster[1], "a word is a speech sound or series of speech sounds that symbolizes and communicates a meaning usually without being divisible into smaller units capable of independent use." However, in my own interpretation, a word is a speech sound that has the power to influence, persuade, explain, and educate. Words are persuasive tools we use in our personal and professional

---

[1] Merriam-Webster

communications daily. Therefore, it is essential to be knowledgeable in how to use our words or all forms of communication effectively. It is your choice to make your words into weapons of mass destruction or vast construction. Now, let's talk shop!

As a not-for-profit organization, external communication methods are incredible ways to share your mission. Communication comes in various forms with various budgets. For example, a conversation with your friends about an upcoming event your organization is hosting is free of cost. Meanwhile, working with a media purchaser to run commercials on your local television and radio stations can be quite costly. While both involve words, each has a very different cost associated. We will discuss these types of costs in Chapter 2 as we learn about the different types of media. Talking positively about your organization is the perfect way to utilize words and communication free of charge. Share new and exciting information with your friends, family members, neighbors, social clubs, and social media accounts. Use these words to your advantage.

Despite the positives, a word is also a speech sound that has the potential to damage, destroy, shame, and humiliate. This means you must be careful and cautious with how you and your organization use words. As easy as they may be to put out there, they're near impossible to retract.

Are you familiar with the story often shared on social media about a mother who imparts a valuable lesson to her children using a tube of toothpaste? In 2016, Amy Beth Gardner posted this photo and accompanying text on Facebook. She details a conversation she had with her daughter on Facebook[2] about the power of words.

---

[2] Amy Beth Gardner, Facebook Page, August 14, 2016.

(Image Credit: Amy Beth Gardner)

"My daughter starts middle school tomorrow. We've decorated her locker, bought new uniforms, even surprised her with a new backpack. But tonight, just before bed, we did another pre-middle school task that is far more important than the others. I gave her a tube of toothpaste and asked her to squirt it out onto a plate. When she finished, I calmly asked her to put all the toothpaste back in the tube. She began exclaiming things like "But I can't!" and "It won't be like it was before!" I quietly waited for her to finish and then said the following:

'You will remember this plate of toothpaste for the rest of your life. Your words have the power of life or death. As you go into middle school, you are about to see just how much weight your words carry. You will have the opportunity to use your words to hurt, demean, slander, and wound others. You are also going to have the opportunity to use your words to heal, encourage, inspire and love others. You will occasionally make the wrong choice; I can think of three times this week I have used my own words carelessly and caused harm. Just like this toothpaste, once the words leave your mouth, you can't take them back. Use your words carefully, Breonna. When others are misusing their words, guard your words. Make the choice every morning that life-giving words will come out of your mouth. Decide tonight that you are going to be a life-giver in middle school. Be known for your gentleness and compassion. Use your life to give life to a world that so desperately needs it. You will never, ever regret choosing kindness."

While this story is a great lesson for children, it's also an important reminder for anyone who works for a business, institution, or organization. Your words reflect you and your employer. When your words are written or spoken to a media outlet, this especially holds true. But, unfortunately, you can rarely take back what you've already stated on record.

###

TIDBIT:

When you or a representative conduct an interview with a media outlet, it is assumed that everything you say to the reporter is on the record. Information you share with them at any point can be considered reportable, unless you preface information with the phrase "off the record," as explained below.

"Off record" or "off the record" are phrases that refer to a statement that is not reportable or not yet reportable. The terms are widely known to be professionally binding and respected in the news industry; however, they are not legally binding. Therefore, it is best practice to use this phrase ahead of any piece of information you are planning to share with a reporter. "Off the record" is often used for a news tip that is not yet officially reportable; however, it may soon be a future topic of discussion. For example: "Off the record, our organization is in the planning stages of purchasing land for a new building next year. Check back with me in a few months for an update, and maybe you can have an exclusive interview announcing the plans to the public."

2

UTILIZING DIFFERENT TYPES OF MEDIA

Understanding the main media categories.

In order to best explain the different types of media, it's common in the public relations industry to categorize media into four types: paid, earned, shared, and owned media. This is also known as the PESO Model, coined by marketing pro, author, and business owner Gini Dietrich in 2014.[3] It's a concept that has been embraced by the public relations community as an all-encompassing way to take the four media types and merge them together.

---

[3] Gini Dietrich, "What is the PESO Model?" *Spin Sucks* (blog). September 8, 2020. https://spinsucks.com/communication/peso-model-breakdown/

Dietrich created this model with an added emphasis on the power of social media through owned and shared media types along with the traditional earned and paid media types.

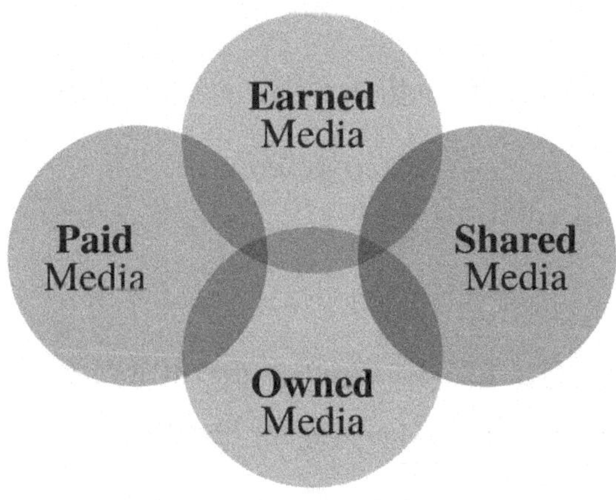

(Graphic adapted from traditional PESO Model)

Paid Media

This type of media is just as it sounds. Paid media is media that is paid for through advertising methods and campaigns. This can be a television commercial, radio ad, promotional segment, sponsored content, social media advertising, etc. Here are a few examples:

- Your nonprofit pays Facebook, LinkedIn, or Instagram to run targeted advertisements or sponsored content
- Your nonprofit hires a local radio station to produce and air an advertisement or commercial
- Your nonprofit works with a local television station for a promotional spot or commercial
- Your nonprofit publishes an advertorial in a newspaper or magazine
- Your nonprofit hires an influencer to post about your organization on social media or on their blog

For many groups, it is beneficial to look for paid media opportunities. If you think this could be something you'd be interested in pursuing, I recommend researching typical budgets for paid media and strategizing how to get the most bang for your buck.

Earned Media

This type of media comes with no cost. It's the media attention that your organization has earned, for free, often through newsworthy story pitches. Through a strong media relations strategy that we'll focus on building through this book, you'll learn techniques for earning as much media as possible. This may be an interview on a local television station, radio station, newspaper article, or magazine. Here are a few examples:

- Your nonprofit is interviewed by a local television station about a recent event or fundraiser you hosted
- Your nonprofit is invited to share information about your organization during a live radio interview
- Your nonprofit is featured in an article in a newspaper or magazine

- Your nonprofit is highlighted in a digital journal or blog

Earned media is the main focus of this book. In the upcoming chapters, we will discuss ways to form professional relationships and partnerships with local media outlets, reporters, hosts, and personalities. I'm a firm believer that the best press is free press.

Shared Media

Shared media is the newest type of media. Based on social media, it's the type of media with a fresh take on how people are getting their news. Shared media refers to what your organization posts on social media and how your organization is represented on these platforms. It also includes being tagged in a social media post, getting a social media shout-out, or having a post shared by others. This type of media comes without a cost. Here are a few examples:

- Your nonprofit posts an update on social media (Facebook, Instagram, Twitter, LinkedIn, etc.)
- Your nonprofit posts an article on Medium
- Your nonprofit posts an announcement on social media (Facebook, Instagram, Twitter, LinkedIn), and it gets shared by your audience
- Your nonprofit is tagged in a post on social media by another account

While we won't focus heavily on social media for nonprofit organizations in this book, it is a type of media that you need to utilize. I recommend that your organization creates and maintains social media accounts frequently used by your target audience. For example, if your target is high schoolers, you may want to create a TikTok and/or Snapchat account. However, if your audience is older, you may consider Facebook and/or LinkedIn. Your organization does not need to create an account on every social media platform. Only create accounts that you can commit to updating, at the very least, a few times a week.

Owned Media

Another type of media that can come without a cost is owned media. This is media that your organization owns through unique creation and page ownership. This is content that is generated for your website, blog, printed newsletter, or magazine. While owned media can be created in-house at no additional cost, hiring an outside full-service marketing agency is not uncommon. Another option is employing a freelance content creator to handle it for you. Even though your organization will own the product, it comes with a cost due to their provided services. This often involves a signed contract agreement and sometimes a retainer. Hiring an agency can significantly benefit your group if there isn't a marketing-savvy staff member or volunteer. Some nonprofits believe that the creative service pays for itself through quality work that leads to an increase in donations. Every organization is unique, and it's certainly not a one-size-fits-all approach. For this specific focus, let's highlight a few no-cost owned media ideas in the examples below:

- Your nonprofit publishes a newsletter that is mailed to donors.
- Your nonprofit creates and publishes its own magazine.
- Your nonprofit writes stories and articles for its website/blog.
- Your nonprofit features testimonials from clients, volunteers, and/or beneficiaries on its website or blog.

Owned media is a great way to reach your audience through your own media forms. While a self-published newsletter or magazine could be a goal for large nonprofits, there are plenty of owned media options for nonprofits of any size. I strongly recommend a blog on an organization's website. This is an opportunity for your nonprofit to share success stories, profile pieces, and self-published articles. If you choose to add blogs to your website, consider setting a realistic goal. While you may want to publish a new blog once a week, it may be more realistic to start by publishing a blog once or twice per month. Keep in mind that if your content is well-researched, it could also turn into earned media if your information is featured on other platforms.

TIDBIT:

As a nonprofit, your organization has endless opportunities for each type of media discussed in the PESO Model. The concept of paid, earned, shared, and owned media types can help your nonprofit reach your target audience to reach your organizational goals. Whether that's an increase in donations or the spread of more awareness, it's essential to understand how this model can help create a solid marketing strategy. While we're focusing on earned media in the forthcoming chapters, I encourage you to research more about paid, shared, and owned media and how these types can benefit your organization. This will also explain how reputation, lead generation, partnerships, and community efforts can assist in the different types of media. For more information about the PESO Model, visit www.spinsucks.com

3

PITCHING FOR VARIOUS PLATFORMS

Media is continuously evolving.

I t is a big undertaking to even begin to explain the different types of media. In today's world of technology, even a social media account without followers can be considered a source of information for reporters and news gatherers. We have seen how viral videos have sparked newsworthy stories. Therefore, it is safe to assume that almost anyone with a cell phone can be considered a resource for a media outlet. As we discuss the direction of your nonprofit's media strategy, let's focus on specific types of media groups and how you can utilize each one to help spread your mission and increase awareness in your communities.

Each media section will conclude with a few content pitch ideas. These are general, but my goal is to spark creativity and ideas for your organization. We will later discuss how to properly pitch stories and content to give your ideas urgency and relevancy. Finally, during the "Pitching a Complete Story Idea" chapter, I'll explain the angles of story pitches that media agencies are looking for in earned coverage opportunities.

Television

Television media consists of broadcast news, network programming, and public access. Broadcast news stations are owned by private media companies and funded through advertisements, network agreements, and programming fees. I've spent nearly 10 years of my professional career working as an anchor and reporter in small to medium-sized television markets. A television market is how cities and areas are ranked based on the number of households with televisions. According to the 2021 Nielsen rankings report[4], there are 210 Designated Market Areas (DMAs). The map below shows the largest TV market, based in New York, and the smallest TV market, based in Montana.

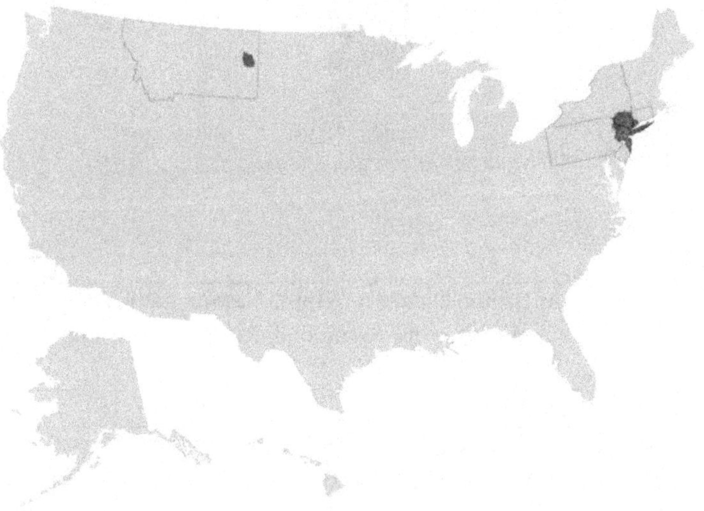

New York, New York is the largest market with 7,452,620 TV homes. According to The Nielsen Company, this DMA is represented by 29 counties in

---

[4] The Nielsen Company DMA Rankings 2021

four states, including New York, Connecticut, New Jersey, and Pennsylvania.

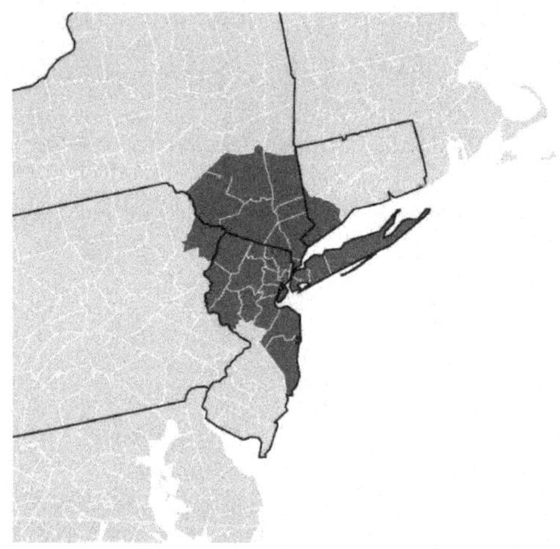

New York: Bronx, Dutchess, Kings, Nassau, New York, Orange, Putnam, Queens, Richmond, Rockland, Suffolk, Sullivan, Ulster, Westchester
Connecticut: Fairfield
New Jersey: Bergen, Essex, Hudson, Hunterdon, Middlesex, Monmouth, Morris, Ocean, Passaic, Somerset, Sussex, Union, Warren
Pennsylvania: Pike

Meanwhile, Glendive, Montana, is the smallest market with 3,900 TV homes. This DMA includes the counties of Dawson and Prairie in the eastern part of Montana.

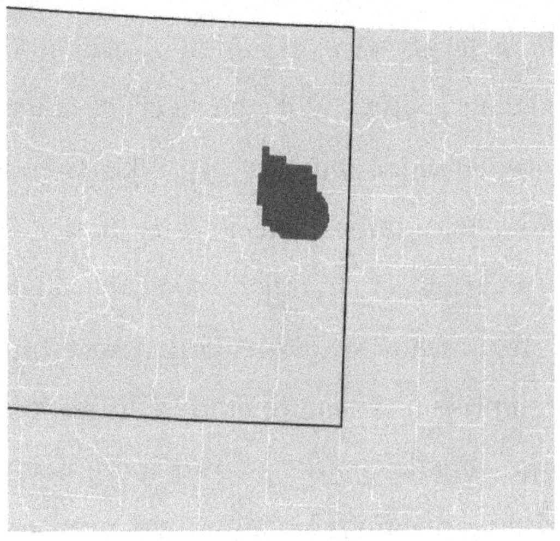

I've spent time in newsrooms of various market sizes, including internships in a top 25 market and a mid-130s market. My career as an anchor and reporter took me to a market in the mid-170s and a market in the low-100s. So why is this critical knowledge for nonprofits? Well, I want you to understand how television news stations choose stories for newscasts and why some markets will give more coverage to nonprofits.

News stations assign reporters to the top stories of the day. Each market has a different expectation of a top story. As an example, we'll assume crime is a top story. In a larger city like New York, it can be expected that reporters will cover a crime story every day. However, in a smaller city, like Glendive, a crime story may only make its way in a newscast once or twice a week. In other words, the smaller the market often means fewer breaking news stories and more enterprise and feature stories. In my personal experience, smaller markets cover more news from nonprofit organizations because they have the extra time in the newscasts to do it. Larger markets will cover nonprofit news, just not as frequently. As a result, they have more breaking news which must make its way into newscasts. This does not mean that larger stations don't find your work essential or valuable. It just may not be as newsworthy and impactful for the station to put it in a newscast.

Television Content Pitch Ideas:
Relevant and exclusive news story pitches
Offer local experts for national/state trending stories
Offer organization opinion/stances for trending controversies
Weekly or monthly segments on specialized topics
Live interviews about upcoming fundraisers and events

Radio

Radio broadcasting in a commercial form has been around for more than a century. Types of radio broadcasting include AM and FM stations, which are made up of subtypes, including commercial radio broadcasting and non-commercial educational radio broadcasting. Commercial broadcasting stations are privately owned and often specialize in news, talk, music, and sports. These stations are funded through advertising to make a profit. Non-commercial educational broadcasting stations are funded by private donations, grants, and/or underwriting. These stations often include public broadcasting, public radio, college radio, and religious broadcasting. According to a 2020 report of broadcast station totals from the Federal Communications Commission (FCC), there are nearly 15,500 radio stations nationwide.[5] While some of these are stations that broadcast nationally, most are local radio stations.

As the industry changes and adapts to new technology like internet radio and satellite radio, listeners consume this type of media differently. While listenership numbers may fluctuate, there are always loyal and local radio listeners. As a way to grow and stabilize in an ever-changing industry, stations will often partner with organizations to host events, supply on-air content, and attract community involvement and interest. This is an opportunity for nonprofits to get involved in local radio station programming by finding ways to pitch their missions and causes. It is often a win-win for various stations which focus on community, entertainment, and talk.

---

[5] Federal Communications Commission, April 5, 2021

For example, radio stations may be interested in a live interview segment that offers their listeners with educational perspective. Keep in mind, their audience is only listening. If you think about when you listen to the radio, it is often while driving, working, or multitasking. This means the best type of pitches are ones that can easily be communicated verbally.

Radio Content Pitch Ideas:
Weekly or monthly segments on specialized topics
Live interviews about upcoming fundraisers and events
Offer opportunities to broadcast live from the organization's facility
Offer opportunities to broadcast live from community outreach events

Print

Newspapers, magazines, and trade publications are the oldest forms of media. Newspapers date back to the 17th century. Hundreds of years later, print media is still being published, yet the industry is struggling. According to the Pew Research Center[6], newspaper circulation and revenue are falling nationwide. In the next graphic, you can see the total circulation of U.S. daily newspapers begins to fall in the late 2000s compared to a steady trend in decades prior.

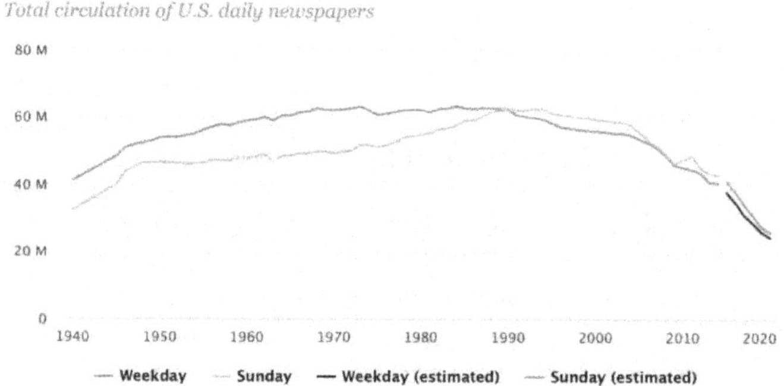

(Graphic from the Pew Research Center. Source: Editor & Publisher (through 2014); estimate based on Pew Research Center analysis of Alliance for Audited Media data 2015-2020).

To make up the difference, many newspapers are cutting costs and raising prices. This includes reducing staff writers and decreasing publishing

---

[6] Pew Research Center, 2020

days. However, in recent years, newspapers have realized opportunities despite the decline in circulation. Many newspapers are making additional revenue through online subscriptions and website advertisements. Traditional advertisements in newspapers are still regularly purchased by businesses and organizations with a target audience of newspaper readers. Yet, an increase in web traffic and digital advertising brings the potential for additional revenue in a new, innovative way. According to research in the below graphic from the Pew Research Center, there is an increase in the number of monthly unique visitors to the websites of the nation's top 50 newspapers by circulation.

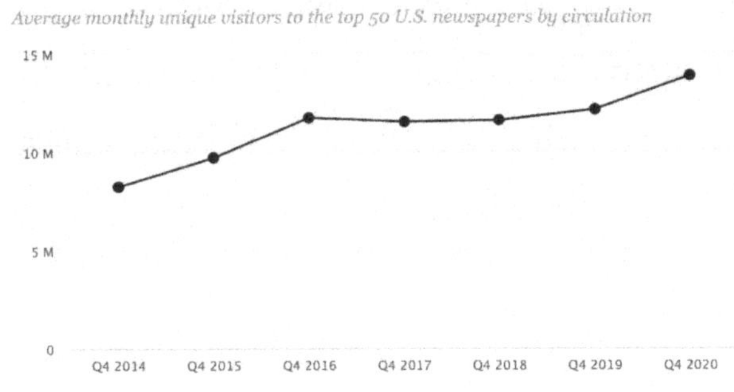

(Graphic from the Pew Research Center. Source: Comscore Media Metrix® Multi-Platform, US, Unique Visitors, October-December 2014-2020)

As the print industry changes, the concept of sharing news does not. Many newspapers include various sections such as local, national, international, sports, feature, lifestyle, business, and classifieds. Magazines and trade publications are in a similar position of losing money and decreasing print frequency. Many are becoming web-based as in electronic magazines or digital magazines.

Nonprofit organizations looking to share their mission through print outlets must do so with a news or feature story angle. When considering a story for a newspaper, consider what is timely and relevant in the world. When considering a story for a feature magazine or trade publication, consider an angle that will captivate a reader with interviews and photos. Remember, while this piece will be read, it must also be visually appealing.

Print Content Pitch Ideas:
Relevant news story pitches in print form
Weekly or monthly op-eds written by editorials with organization representatives
Offer local experts for national/state trending stories
Offer organization opinion/stances for trending controversies
Give photos with captions of recent events and fundraisers

Digital

The newest and fastest-growing media form, digital media, is consumed electronically. Digital media outlets include the internet, social media, podcasts, video sharing, streaming services, and smartphone apps. Most television, radio, and print outlets also have a digital media component. Many television, radio, and print outlets will also use digital media elements to expand viewership, listenership, and readership. Their goal is often to attract a new audience that wouldn't otherwise watch the news, listen to the radio, or read a newspaper. Therefore, on a digital platform, these news outlets may include stories that they would not typically consider for broadcast or print.

Unlike television and radio stations, digital media has no time limit. This means content can be produced for a 30-second video clip on Instagram or a 30-minute feature segment on YouTube. Also, unlike newspapers and magazines, digital media does not have a maximum or minimum word count. This allows a lot of opportunity for creativity with story ideas and content pitches. While these digital outlets are looking to generate money with content, they will also see value in working with a nonprofit organization to expand their reach.

Digital Content Pitch Ideas:
Relevant and exclusive news story pitches
Recurring segment through the web or social media
Interview on a local podcast or digital talk show
Offer local expert interviews for trending news stories

Social media account takeover
Behind the scenes tour of the facility
Guest vlog or blog by an organization staff member/volunteer

###

TIDBIT:

As you learn more about the different types of media outlets, I want you to recognize their work and treat them as the individual outlets they are. In this politically charged environment, the media is criticized for various reasons. All too often, the criticism is directed at an outlet that had nothing to do with the initial issue or controversy. Whether it's considered justified, remember that your nonprofit organization should stay unbiased toward issues that do not directly impact your organization. It's fair to consider that if you want "the media" to respect you and your organization, don't bash "the media" as an entity. If you have an issue with one particular source or a concern about a particular news story, you should address it directly with the outlet responsible. I've seen many situations where a nonprofit employee chooses to publicly bash "the media" as a whole. This usually ended poorly for the nonprofit since the local TV stations, newspapers, and radio stations felt attacked. If you say or write something insulting toward "the media" as a whole, don't expect the media, which includes your local television and radio stations, to help your organization promote an upcoming event, fundraiser, or announcement. Respect is a two-way street.

4

IMPLEMENTING A PLAN FOR MEDIA INQUIRIES

Always be available to the media.

Not-for-profit organizations are commonly approached for various media interviews, stories, and comments. Oftentimes, these nonprofit groups offer a professional opinion and informative point-of-view. Most news agencies would rather give news attention to a nonprofit rather than a business or corporation. Nonprofits are frequently trusted as reliable sources because of their efforts in the community. Generally speaking, nonprofits are working toward a common good. Outlets would prefer to give coverage to a charity providing public benefit rather than a company looking to attract more for-profit business. That said, if approached for a positive story, your organization shouldn't turn it down or appear unorganized. If a media outlet is offering you an interview opportunity, you need to take it. If an outlet is contacting you for more information about an event, you need to provide it. Frequently, media outlets will contact an organization and need an interview, quotes, or statement within just a few hours. In these instances, organizations should be flexible with this standard. Below are suggestions for developing and implementing a media inquiry plan.

Assume a Media Contact

Your media relations contact will depend on the size of your organization. Suppose your organization has a national reach with dozens of employees. In that case, you may have a full-time position dedicated to marketing, public relations, and/or communication. If your organization is small with a hyper-local impact, you may have just a couple employees or operate on a complete volunteer or board member basis. To determine which format is best for your organization, have a conversation with your staff members and board of directors to choose a point person to handle media inquiries. If a news agency reaches out to the organization, this person will handle all communication and interview coordination. They can be interviewed or they can set up interviews for others.

When choosing a contact person, make sure they are qualified to handle media interviews. This person should be comfortable with public speaking and stay composed, yet energetic and passionate. During the interview, they must be able to speak well, in a clear and concise manner. This person should also be able to put industry phrases and jargon into everyday conversation. The general public probably won't understand industry terminology, so it's best to keep the language straightforward.

It's also essential to have a secondary, and if necessary, a third point person for media relations. If your organization's primary point person is out of the office or unavailable, have a backup. Then, have a backup for the backup. This can be another staff member or board member. These representatives should have similar communication qualifications. They should also be knowledgeable about the organization, the topic of the interview, and the subject matter.

Develop a Policy

Develop a communication plan if a reporter or media representative contacts your organization through a general email or phone number. Each staff member or volunteer should know the course of action to get this reporter in contact with your primary point person. If that person is unavailable, staff members should know to move on to the organization's secondary and third options.

Your organization may be interested in going a step further by creating a formal media policy for media outlets. This policy would get distributed to your media networks, which explains your organization's expectations for them. This can address topics like:

- Information on how to request an interview
- Details on after-hours requests, if applicable
- Your organization's media relations representative
- Official spokesperson(s) for your organization

Developing and implementing a policy pertaining to media relations will ensure that everyone understands your organization's expectations regarding external communications.

Utilize Your Website

If your organization has a website, consider adding a page dedicated to media relations. If I'm a member of the media and I'm looking to contact an organization, the first thing I'll do is scroll to the bottom of a webpage. The footer will likely have basic information and quick links that include topics such as contact information, organization history, location, or careers. It's becoming increasingly popular for organizations to include a link in their footer or in their page navigation that's geared toward the media. This tab or link is often titled "press room" or "media inquiries." On this page, a reporter can expect to find recent press releases and media relations contacts. This concept can be utilized for an organization of any size.

Within my research, I have noticed many nonprofit websites with a page dedicated specifically to media and press. On this page, I can expect to find recent press releases and media relations contacts. This concept can be utilized for an organization of any size.

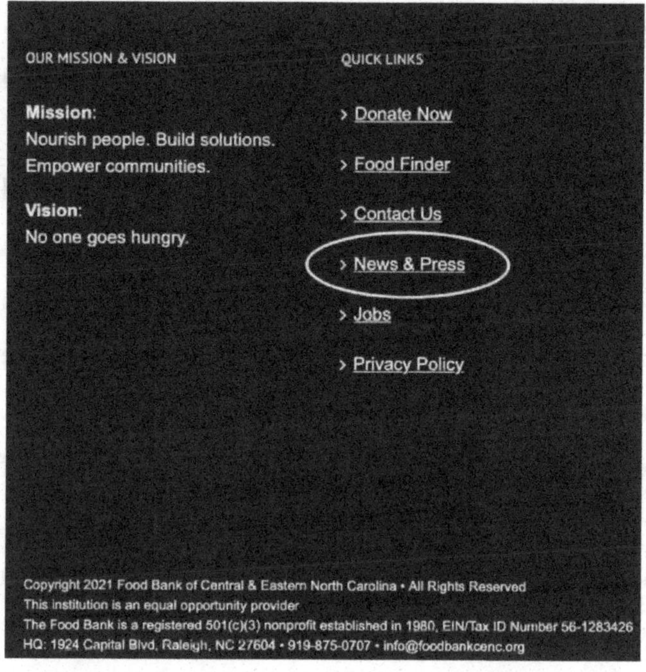

(Image credit: The Food Bank of Central & Eastern North Carolina,
https://foodbankcenc.org)

As an example, the Food Bank of Central & Eastern North Carolina does a great job of this on its website.[7] In the footer of its website, there is a section called "Quick Links," which includes a link for "News & Press." Once clicked, this link takes the

---

[7] The Food Bank of Central & Eastern North Carolina, https://foodbankcenc.org

user to a page that features contacts for media relations, recent press releases, news articles, and downloadable logo formats. Through this link in the footer and on the media-focused webpage, the Food Bank of Central & Eastern North Carolina allows the media to quickly and easily access the information and contacts that they need. For this reason alone, be sure to keep your organization's website current. Reporters will often research organizations ahead of time and look for supplemental information online. In addition, they may use statistics, data, and material from your website or FAQs section, so make sure it is up-to-date.

Monitor Social Media

Social media accounts have become a new form of public relations and communication. What you post on social media may get the attention of the media. Include your organization's preferred contact information, including an email address on your social media accounts. This ensures reporters can find these details with ease. Despite including your preferred method of communication, members of the media may end up contacting you in other ways, including direct messaging on Facebook, Instagram, Twitter, and LinkedIn. Be sure that staff members are checking these inboxes frequently and passing along inquiries to your point person.

If your organization is readily available to the media, the media will often make coverage available to your organization. I'm sure that most nonprofits will agree that the best type of publicity is free publicity through earned media.

TIDBIT:

As you've likely realized from reading this chapter, sometimes interview requests from the media require quick turnarounds. This can be anywhere from a few minutes to a few hours. I'm not proud to admit this, but back in my reporting days, I can't tell you the number of times I would unexpectedly stop by a local nonprofit's office to ask if someone was available for an interview. While it wasn't my preferred interview set-up method, sometimes it was all that my deadline would allow. The nonprofits that invited me in with just a few minutes' notice and were happy to do an interview made my job much easier that day.

Meanwhile, on an ideal reporting day, I'd have the flexibility to set up interviews ahead of time, either for later that day or possibly the next day. Still, that timeframe is rarely ideal for a busy nonprofit organization. Now that I'm in a professional marketing and communications role, I know how challenging it can be to receive a last-minute interview request. However, due to my background in news, I know that it's worth the trouble. Suppose your nonprofit is able to set up an interview for a media outlet on short notice. In that case, they'll keep coming back to you for other interviews in the future.

The easier you make it for them, the more they will want to work with you and your organization.

Read that again: The easier you make it for them (being reporters and journalists), the more they will want to work with you and your organization. That means more earned media for your nonprofit.

5

LEARNING THE INDUSTRY LINGO

Speak the language of the media.

As with any industry, the media has its own language. These unique phrases and terms are often used behind the scenes, so you may never hear them. There will, however, be occasions when you're involved in the conversation and need to determine your organization's best coverage option. In this chapter, we will explain several common phrases, how they're used, and how your organization can use them too.

Live Interview

Some outlets like television, radio, and even digital media offer live interview opportunities. These types of interviews are live during a broadcast. In the way of television, these spots are typically anywhere from two to five minutes. Live interviews are most common for nonprofit groups during a morning news broadcast or during a lifestyle show. As for radio, these segments may be a little longer and can be done with different hosts based on their programming and preferences. As digital media continues to grow, live interviews are becoming popular via social media like Facebook Live, Live on Instagram, and YouTube Live. I'm sure it won't take long before more platforms create live video features.

Interview

An interview in a non-live format applies to all outlets. This is a broad concept and can be utilized by television, radio, print, and digital platforms. In television, this interview will likely be prerecorded on camera, virtually through video conference, or by phone. A prerecorded interview in radio, will typically be conducted over the phone or in-studio. For a podcast, you may have a virtual video conference or be in the studio. In print, this interview will probably be a conversation over the phone or in person. If the interview is done in person, you'll likely see a digital recorder. Then, direct quotes will be used in a newspaper or magazine. In digital, interviews can be done through any of the above formats. It is best to research the type of interviews done by each outlet if your organization is asked to provide an interview or comment. If you're pitching a story, you should already have an idea of how the outlet will want to capture an interview.

Editorial

An editorial is an opinionated article traditionally seen in print journalism, such as in newspapers and magazines. As media platforms evolved over the years, editorials can also be found in television, radio, and digital outlets. The publishing of editorials depends on the circumstances and content guidelines of the particular outlet. Fitting to its name, an editorial is an opinion piece written or announced by an editor at the news organization. This piece expresses the organization's view on a specific subject or topic that may be controversial.

Op-Ed

Similar to an editorial, an op-ed is another type of opinion piece. Op-eds feature the opinion of a guest writer. The name comes from where and how they were originally printed, which was on the page opposite from the editorials. Op-eds are still common in print media and are becoming increasingly popular throughout digital platforms. You may benefit from contributing op-eds to a local newspaper, magazine, or digital news outlet as a nonprofit organization. These could be beneficial ways to address the issues your organization faces or the work you do to combat issues in the community.

Enterprise Story

Frequently television, radio, and print outlets will look for local feature stories or enterprise stories. In the industry, enterprise stories are referred to as story ideas that are originally created and individually produced by an outlet or reporter. Enterprise stories are not based on a press release or promoted event. These stories are usually exclusive to the particular station, newspaper, or magazine that generated them.

Evergreen Story

Similar to an enterprise story, an evergreen story is a unique type of feature story. This is a topic that will maintain its value over time. For instance, these stories can be utilized at any time rather than a story tied to a specific date or deadline. Evergreen stories won't lose relevance as time goes on. Sometimes, once published, these types of stories are shared for years. This is because the story is just as powerful two years later as it was when it was published. While many news outlets prioritize timely and relevant news stories, evergreen stories still have a place in the news. These types of stories can be pitched when there is an opportunity to share a human-interest story or feature story that will draw readers, viewers, and/or listeners.

Exclusive

This is a great word to keep in your vocabulary as a nonprofit organization. An "exclusive" means there is a news story that is only given to one specific organization. Media outlets love the term "exclusive" because it means they'll be the only news organization to have the story. Offering an exclusive story or interview to a particular reporter or news outlet will help your nonprofit group build professional news relationships. In addition, these valuable and highly sought-after exclusive stories will allow you to leverage your content. We'll discuss this topic more in Chapter 10: Creating a Lasting Partnership.

TIDBIT:

Let's talk about press conferences. These types of events are often organized by government entities, law enforcement agencies, and politicians. However, they aren't limited to only those groups. Nonprofit organizations can certainly host a press conference, commonly known as a media conference or news conference. For example, suppose your organization has something big to announce. In that case, it could be beneficial to host a press conference where your group shares information and takes questions. Now, it's important to note that not all announcements deserve a press conference. For example, while adding a new staff member is exciting to you, it may not be worthy of a full press conference. However, the announcement of your groundbreaking of a new facility could be considered a press conference opportunity. Therefore, when you send out an alert to your media contacts, be sure to include the date, time, location, and give a brief overview of the announcement that will be discussed.

6

PITCHING A COMPLETE STORY IDEA

Your pitch will make or break coverage.

To get coverage of the important and passionate work that your organization is doing, you need to pitch your story. You can do this by brainstorming your organization's recent accomplishments and humanizing them through various elements used for different types of media outlets. I created a formula that will help your organization formulate a story pitch. This is called the **STRONG** method and features the components of a story pitch that will attract coverage. The **STRONG** method includes sharing a problem or issue in your community, telling the details on how your organization is working to help combat that problem or issue; raising awareness for your organization; offering a humanizing component to the pitch; noting statistics, numbers, and/or research to back up the pitch; and giving a call to action to let the audience know what they should do or take away from the story.

Steps for a STRONG Story Pitch

S hare a problem/issue in your community

T ell the details on your efforts to help

R aise awareness for your mission

O ffer a humanizing component

N ote statistics, numbers, or research

G ive a call to action

Below are a few examples of nonprofit missions in homelessness, animal rescue, and substance abuse. Before we jump in, I want to point out the importance of confidentiality and permissions. For the following story pitches, let's assume that the organizations have already completed the process of receiving permission from their representatives to offer the humanizing component. Many nonprofits, perhaps yours included, keep their work private due to the nature of their mission. Therefore, it is essential that you receive prior permission from any individual or family you've served before pitching their story to the media. Keep that in mind as you look at these pitches that are complete ideas and share the following aspects of a **STRONG** method story pitch:

How has your organization helped the homeless population? Introduce the audience to someone who is back on their feet and credits your organization for providing them with shelter, food, clothing, education, and/or fellowship. Coordinate a media interview with this person to share their personal story. Offer an additional interview with a nonprofit representative who will provide additional elements for the story, such as factual information about homeless statistics and the impact your organization has in the region.

How has your organization saved the life of a dog or cat? Introduce the media to the animal's new family and share why they chose to adopt. Set up an interview with the family and their rescued pet. Be sure that the location for the interview will allow for active visuals of the pet and its family. Have a staff member available for an interview about the importance of animal rescue and spay/neuter efforts. Ensure they are knowledgeable about current regional statistics regarding cat and dog overpopulation and euthanasia. This type of story will tug at heartstrings and create a memorable experience for the audience.

How has your organization worked to decrease substance abuse in the community? Introduce the reader to a family willing to share their emotional story. Perhaps the family was brought back together thanks to sobriety. Perhaps the family is helping others because they lost a loved one to an overdose. Have a conversation with the family before pitching the interview about what they are willing to share. Ask for family photos and videos to help tell their story and put a personifying touch on a tough subject. Consider having an organization representative present during the interview to provide information about the nonprofit's mission and how it works to help individuals and families.

When you're ready to send your pitch, make sure that your media contact list is up-to-date. I recommend revising your contact lists once a month. Stay current with new reporters when they come to the market and remove former reporters who left the market. You can often find reporter's emails on the media outlet's website. In addition, you can connect with reporters on their professional social media platforms like their Facebook fan pages and public Instagram accounts. Be sure to reach out to them through their public profile or work email rather than their private accounts or personal emails.

TIDBIT:

As a former journalist, I believe that a well-written release is the most effective way to communicate specific details of a topic, issue, event, etc., to the community, newsroom, or publication. How your release is written can determine if it gets media attention. Your press release writer should think like a journalist and answer the basic topics of who, what, where, when, why, and how (5WHs). In addition, be sure this press release is written with proper spelling, grammar, and usage. If applicable, the writer of the release can also include quotes from a staff member or board member. Quotes are often used to share feelings and impact. Meanwhile, the body text of a release is used to share factual information and the basic topics of the 5WHs.

By the way, if you're wondering why the content of each chapter in this book ends with three pound symbols/number signs, it is relative to the press release format. The "###" is a way to let the audience know that their press release has come to an end. It's not certain how this originated, but historians believe it could date back to telegraphic shorthand in the Civil War era. Once the body content of the press release has come to an end, it's typical to see ### centered, on the next line down. Below that, you may see a boilerplate statement. While it's not necessary that your organization follows this format for your press releases, it is common in the public relations industry. Personally,

I like the "###" feature and I think it adds a bit of character to the formatting of a press release.

7

PREPARING FOR AN INTERVIEW

Share your message with clarity and confidence.

Congratulations! You've secured an interview with a media outlet! This might be a phone call interview, a virtual on-camera interview, an in-person on-camera interview, or a radio interview. To get ready for this interview, you'll need to prepare. This reminds me of the 5Ps of success: proper planning prevents poor performance. No matter the media platform for your interview, the preparation will be similar.

As a media relations expert with a background in journalism, I recommend creating an outline ahead of the interview. Include notes about your topic, details about the research, and list any relevant numbers or statistics. You can keep this on hand to reference if you need to during the interview. While reporters generally don't offer questions ahead of time, it doesn't hurt to ask. You can send them an email that says something like:

"As I get ready for our interview, I want to make sure I have the most updated information and relevant facts to help further your story. Are you able to send me a few questions ahead of time so I can prepare?"

They may send a few questions, or they may not. Either way, you can still nail the interview without preparing responses. Here are a few more suggestions to help you effectively share your message and expertise:

Introduce Yourself

At the very beginning of a newspaper or television interview, reporters will often ask you to say and spell your first and last name for their records. They may also ask for your title. If they don't ask for this information, offer it to them. Pronounce your name and spell it out slowly and clearly. This will ensure that your name is correct when published or broadcasted. If you have a business card, it's also a good idea to share that with them too.

This may not be necessary if you're a live guest on a television broadcast or radio segment. In those situations, the interviewer will likely introduce you to the audience prior to asking you questions. During live interviews, you'll want to give them a brief biography ahead of time, so they introduce you properly and share the correct information about your organization.

Know Your Interviewer

Just like your interviewer will research you and your organization, you should research them too. Read or watch some of their previous stories. Knowing their reporting style can help you prepare for the type of story they'll share about your organization.

If you're a live guest on a news program or radio show segment, do some research about the format. For example, find out how long the interview will last, how many questions they'll ask, and what other guests have discussed during past interview segments.

Complete Your Sentences

Once you start talking, sometimes it's hard to keep your sentences complete and brief. I know this all too well, especially when I'm excited about something. Even with professional training, I still have to coach myself to slow down, enunciate, and stick to short sentences. While it may be difficult to remember in the moment, try to finish each sentence rather than rushing into the next one. Broadcast and radio journalists often choose quotes (or soundbites) from interviews that run about 10 to 15 seconds. These quotes can range from 20 to 40 words in print and digital, depending on the article's length. These estimates vary, but each journalist, no matter their platform, will appreciate brevity.

Speak with Confidence

Remember that you're the expert on your subject matter. They wouldn't interview you about your efforts or organization if you were not knowledgeable. So while it's normal to be nervous, I want you to also be confident. Be yourself during an interview, and even though you're talking to a reporter, remember that it's really just a conversation between you and them. So, go ahead and relax, have fun, and share your passion.

Be Honest

If you don't know the answer to a question, that's okay. Just say something like: "I'm not quite sure about that specific detail, and I don't want to give inaccurate information. I'll research it and follow up with you."

I am sure you have seen an interview where the person was asked a question that made them uncomfortable. Or the question seemed off-topic. If you are asked this type of question, do not respond, "no comment." That phrase in the news media has a negative connotation and often makes it seem as if someone is hiding something. While that's often not the case, it's a phrase that should be avoided. Of course, you can always revert back to your original topic or give the question a positive spin. For instance, let's say a reporter asks a question about a controversial issue affecting the nonprofit; a response could be:

"I'm not able to discuss that right now... but I can assure the community that our knowledgeable and talented nonprofit team is doing everything in their power to ensure a positive outcome."

Give Supplemental Information

If you have additional information or data in the form of a brochure, document, or flyer, this could be helpful to the reporter. Consider giving them a folder with information inside of it to help them tell their story. In the public relations world, this is called a media kit. You can include your mission statement and organizational background information. The reporter may use these details when writing their report. I know first-hand that having this information readily accessible is greatly appreciated.

As you prepare for the interview, remember that the reporter is the one telling the story. They will come up with the questions, and when you agree to an interview, that means you agree to answer their questions. Don't tell them what they should ask you or try to control the interview. That can create a negative interview experience and reduce the likeliness that you'll be approached again by that outlet to speak about your organization.

Follow Up

Once you're done with your interview, follow up to ask if the reporter needs any supplemental information or additional comment for their story. After the story is published, be sure to review it. In the event that there is an error in the story, politely address it. I can promise you that I've never come across a media outlet that maliciously misquotes. As a journalist, I understand that mistakes happen, and they can certainly be frustrating for all involved. If you notice a mistake or error in your story, contact the reporter. If you don't get a timely response, then you should consider reaching out to the editor, manager, or news director. Let them know the error, where it is found in the story, and how it can be corrected.

###

TIDBIT:

Many of your interviews may last anywhere from five minutes to 30 minutes. The reporter will often choose the best soundbites or quotes from this interview. While the information you are sharing is important and appreciated, your interview will be significantly shortened in order to fit in their time limit and word count. A typical broadcast news story runs between 20 to 90 seconds which can include interviews, video, and/or reporter track. A typical newspaper article runs between 250 to 600 words, while a magazine piece may include more than 1,000 words. As an interviewee, try to be understanding when your interview is shortened and know that it is not personal.

8

NETWORKING WITH JOURNALISTS

Find a journalist who can relate to your cause.

A common challenge for nonprofit organizations is figuring out the best way to share their missions and visions with the public. As a nonprofit board member and former news anchor, I've learned that one of the best ways to get noticed is actually quite simple. Through networking and connecting with media outlets and their journalists, you can build effective and professional relationships. Keep in mind that these connections should be meaningful and sincere. While you have an ultimate goal of getting positive news coverage and raising awareness about your organization, you want to ensure that your outreach efforts, follow-ups, and responses are genuine.

Take time to research on-air talent at your local television and radio stations and reporters at newspapers and magazines. That means following them on social media and seeing their interests. You can learn a lot from a quick glance at someone's social media account. For instance, if you look at my Facebook and Instagram profiles, you can easily figure out the following:

1. I adopted my dog through a local animal rescue facility.
2. My mom is a breast cancer survivor.
3. I regularly take walks through local parks.

Due to these types of posts on my social media accounts, you can safely assume the following:

1. I support animal rescue efforts since I chose to adopt my dog from a local shelter.
2. I understand the impact cancer can have on a family since my mom had breast cancer.
3. I enjoy exercise and appreciate our local parks and recreation facilities.

All of the above statements are absolutely true. These experiences have resulted in my personal involvement and/or financial support for several local animal rescues, cancer support initiatives, and local environmental recreation groups. Over the years, I've reached out to some local nonprofits and asked how to get involved because I'm passionate about their cause. That said, I've had other organizations reach out to me. Personally, I always appreciated that initiative because it showed that people were watching my work.

When representatives from those organizations introduced themselves, they often just wanted to share their mission, invite me to an upcoming event, or ask if I'd be interested in learning more. Most of the time, I agreed to stop by an event or fundraiser. When I was a news anchor, I knew that my words on-air, online, and in-person were powerful because I was given a platform and a voice. So, if those organizations had a cause that I was passionate about, I was honored to help them get exposure. Personally, I was always happy to give them a shout-out on social media or share details about an upcoming fundraiser.

If you reach out to a local journalist, make sure you have common interests and goals. You want this person to genuinely care about your organization's mission. Too often, nonprofits will reach out to popular anchors or reporters without purpose. They want a well-known person to sit on the board of directors or want a recognizable emcee for an event. Unfortunately, they don't do the background information to see if that person has a vested interest in their cause. Here are a few examples of events/organizations that I didn't get involved with and why:

1. I was asked to be on a planning committee for a local parental support nonprofit. While, of course, I admire and appreciate mothers and fathers in my community, I'm not yet a parent. At this point in my life, I can't relate to them. There were other reporters and anchors in this local news market who have children and are more understanding of this group's mission.

2. A community development commission for a town asked me to chair the area revitalization committee. While I support the growth of small towns in North Carolina, this was not a good fit because I don't live nearby or own property in this region. While I would look forward to the opportunity to visit and explore the community, I wouldn't be a good

resource for the town's development or the best person to chair this committee. So instead, I suggested they ask one of the local bureau reporters who live in that area and know the community.

3. I was asked to emcee a local Latin heritage nonprofit event and facilitate a bilingual community conversation. As someone who is not Spanish-speaking, this would have been a very challenging event for me to host. While I would love to attend the event as an educational opportunity and to support the Latino community, I would not be a proficient emcee. I used this opportunity to direct the group to a bilingual reporter who is passionate about their Latin heritage. He was thrilled to work with them.

If you network with news personalities who are passionate about your mission, the rest should easily fall into place.

###

TIDBIT:

You may notice that news personalities are constantly coming and going in your community. Turnover can be quite high in the news industry. So, unfortunately, it's common for journalists to work in contract cycles and move around. That means that a journalist who you know and trust may not stick around for more than two years. If that's the case, be sure to network and form professional relationships with more than one journalist. If your favorite source is leaving, ask them to introduce you to another reporter or personality. This is a great way to build your network and get "in" with a newer journalist who is also looking to build connections.

9

RECRUITING AN

EMCEE OR HOST

Choose a passionate voice for your event.

Once you create a list of the local journalists or personalities who are passionate and interested in your organization and cause, you'll have options for potential emcees or hosts. Make sure that your emcee choices are already familiar with your organization and your mission. Then, work with your event committee or event chair to rank your top three talent choices.

In terms of timeframe, you'll want to start your emcee search at least three months before your event. When you're ready to make your offers, reach out to your top choice first to see if they're interested in emceeing or hosting your event. This initial email can be pretty basic, but you'll want to include the following information:

- Date of the event
- Time of the event
- What time the emcee/host should arrive
- What is expected of them during the event
- Expected attire/dress code for the event

If your top choice says yes to the emcee opportunity, then you can follow up with more specifics. If they are unavailable for your event, don't take it personally. Media personalities may have conflicts due to their work schedule or because of other commitments. Repeat the process with your second choice, and if necessary, your third choice.

Once you've secured an emcee, offer to meet them in person to discuss the event and their involvement. Over the years, I've had many incredible emcee opportunities, but unfortunately, there were also some bad experiences as well. Here's a list of suggestions to ensure a positive experience for your emcee:

Admission and Ticketing

It is essential that your organization provides complimentary admission/ticketing to your emcee. While this may seem like a no-brainer… I'm going to address it anyway. I've personally emceed two events where I was expected to purchase my own ticket. Since I was already volunteering my time and talent, I was a tad bit shocked. However, I do understand how many organizations may be running off a lower budget. If this is your current situation, just rethink your event structure and see where you can cut costs in other areas. Instead of bringing in a media personality, consider having a volunteer or board member serve as the emcee or host instead.

In addition to covering your emcee's ticket price, it's a wonderful gesture to offer them another complimentary ticket so they can bring a guest. These events were always my favorite because I was able to bring my husband along, and we had a great time together.

In October 2017, I emceed an event for the Young Professionals of Pitt County called "Wiggin' Out for Charity" – hence the pink wigs in the photo. Proceeds from the event benefited a new cancer center at our local medical center. The organization generously covered the cost of my admission and also offered me an additional complimentary ticket, allowing me to bring my then-boyfriend, who is now my husband. We had a fantastic evening networking with health care leaders and other young professionals.

To show our support and appreciation, we made personal donations to the charity to cover the cost of our complimentary tickets and to help support their fundraising efforts.

Reserve Parking

You'll want to make your emcee's attendance and logistics of getting there as easy as possible. If your event is being held in a location where parking is hard to find, consider having a space reserved for them. You can usually work with event venues to make this happen. Suppose parking has a cost associated with it, like in a garage or valet. In that case, I recommend validating their parking ticket or offering to cover their valet expenses.

Araksya Karapetyan, a well-known news anchor in Los Angeles, shared this image on Instagram[8] in November 2014, ahead of an event she attended.

---

[8] Araksya Karapetyan, [@araksyakarapetyan] Photo of parking reserved parking. Instagram, published by Araksya Karapetyan, 26 Nov. 2014, https://www.instagram.com/p/v2hjjND9S8

Reserving a parking space for an emcee or guest of honor is a thoughtful gesture that is much appreciated. This is incredibly refreshing in larger cities or events with limited parking availability.

Event Preparation

Be sure to keep your emcee in the loop as you prepare for the event and solidify the timeline. If your emcee is serving as a true master of ceremonies, provide a script in addition to an outline of the event. I recommend getting this to them at least a week before the event. They'll need plenty of time to look over it and rehearse. It also allows an opportunity for them to ask questions, get name pronunciations, and make changes. It's important to remember that it is not their job as an emcee to write the event script. This needs to be done by your organization to ensure a positive experience.

Promotional Materials

Including your emcee's name and/or photograph in your promotional materials is a nice touch and certainly will make an emcee feel valued. In addition, if your organization is sending invitations, consider adding their name to the text description. For example, it could read something like:

"Our organization is excited to have Maria Satira serve as our emcee for this year's event."

Or

"This year's event will be emceed by Maria Satira, the morning anchor of [insert call letters] News."

You can also use this format on flyers and graphics for social media. If you want to use their photo in promotional materials, ask them to send you their most recent headshot. This ensures that the photo you're using is approved by them and their media company. Before distributing your materials, send a draft to your emcee so they can proof it and make any corrections. Personally, I've lost track of how many times I've seen my name misspelled on promotional materials. Having a second set and even a third set of eyes on this type of content will help ensure it is free of errors.

Having a media personality as an emcee is a true benefit to your organization since they likely have a loyal following and elevated platform. In fact, you may find that having a well-known emcee can help generate even more donations for your organization. Your emcee may share the event on their social media platforms or during their broadcasts, shows, or stories. In addition, community members may purchase tickets because they want to meet your emcee or hear them speak.

TIDBIT:

As with anyone who volunteers or donates their time to your organization, you need to say thank you. Those words go a long way and should be communicated often. If you really want to make a positive impression with your host or emcee following the event, consider sending a thank you card or email. While not always necessary, some organizations go above and beyond with their thank-you efforts. Gifts of appreciation like floral arrangements, goodie baskets, gift certificates, etc., are always memorable. If there is a follow-up email or event recap newsletter, be sure to include a thank you to your emcee in that as well and send them a copy. The more memorable a thank you is, the more likely the emcee or host will work with you or your organization again in the future.

10

CREATING A LASTING PARTNERSHIP

Maintain a professional relationship with the media.

Forming a positive relationship with reporters and news outlets is a great way to maintain your media relations strategy. As you meet and network with reporters, personalities, and talent, keep in contact with them in various ways. Here are a few sincere and thoughtful ideas:

- Reach out via email to offer a compliment on a recent story that you enjoyed

- Follow them on social media and positively engage with their posts

- Ensure that they're on your press release distribution list
- Reach out to them directly with exclusive story ideas
- Check in with them often to share newsworthy information
- Send them a holiday card from your organization
- Mail them your annual report and invitations to fundraisers

As we talked about previously, news reporters and personalities come and go, especially in smaller markets. If this is the case, ask them to introduce you to someone else as their media outlet so you can build a professional relationship with several reporters or talents.

In addition to developing those professional relationships with reporters, it is crucial to establish a partnership with a media outlet's management and leadership. This can range from the general manager, vice presidents, department heads, account executives, or marketing team. These individuals are critical to your ongoing media relations partnership. Keeping a strong connection with them will allow your organization to have recognition in various ways. This can include promotional spots, assisted fundraisers, volunteer opportunities, or other types of partnerships.

TIDBIT:

It's common for news reporters/anchors, journalists, and on-air personalities to have social media accounts for community members to follow. If you're active on social media, you may benefit from following these pages and interacting with them. A few examples could include leaving a comment, sending a message, or sharing a post. This is an easy way to keep in touch with your news contacts and media personalities. When they see your name on social media, they will associate you with encouragement, positivity, and support. When you have that type of name recognition, they'll likely remember you when they're looking for a story idea or story pitch. Remember, you want your media connections to view you and your organization as a resource to them as much as you view them as a resource to your organization.

CONCLUSION

A successful, professional relationship with media outlets can create endless opportunities for your organization. Through consistent and positive media exposure, your organization can flourish. In addition to creating awareness around your organization and mission, you can also gain support through financial donations, supplies donations, and additional volunteers. Creating a lasting partnership with media outlets is truly a win-win for all involved.

If you need guidance with media relations for your nonprofit organization, I'm happy to chat with you.

As a reader of this guide, I'm offering a free 15-minute consultation and/or discussion about your goals. In addition, I can help point you in the right direction and offer unique ideas geared toward your organization.

I've been honored to work alongside several groups and offer insight into their media relations and digital marketing goals. Here's what some nonprofit leaders are saying about our consultations, presentations, and partnerships:

"Our consult with Maria was just the extra boost our startup needed. Because of her marketing savvy, she offered insights and ideas that couldn't be found by simply Googling or reading business books. Her advice and expertise have been invaluable to us."

- Molly Ortiz and Amanda Wall, Founders of a financial literacy nonprofit

###

"The Humane Society of Eastern Carolina was struggling with marketing and media relations until Maria came along. Her wide-ranging knowledge of marketing, promotions, press releases, and use of social media has made all the difference in our organization's presence in the community. Our revenue has gone up substantially with her efforts and talent. The Humane Society of Eastern Carolina will be indebted to her forever."

- Martina Christie, President of the Humane Society of Eastern Carolina

"Maria is consistently smart, professional, creative, and is never afraid of a challenge. She is committed to creating unique and impactful messaging for our current donors as well as the important cultivation of new supporters. In addition, she is providing critical coaching to help us strengthen our "brand" within the community. We are quite fortunate to

have her support and look forward to a long and prosperous partnership."

- Lynn Pischke, Chief Operating Officer of Riley's Army, Inc.

###

"Maria is creative and enthusiastic while also offering realistic and factual information about communicating with the media. She succinctly helped parents learn how to get a main point across by speaking in sound bites, taking a moment to think, and creatively delivering their message with each answer. The topics she covered were relevant in that they were timely and related to topics parents were particularly interested in. She brought a personal touch, letting the group know about her own passions, and how she understands what it is like to talk to the media about something you care deeply about. She built a quick rapport with attendees and

offered a program which was not only informative.
but lasting."

- Kylene Dibble, Executive Director of
Parents for Public Schools of Pitt County

###

Thank you for reading this introductory guide on media relations for nonprofit organizations. I hope you can use this book as a resource to strengthen and enhance your media relations techniques. I genuinely appreciate your hard work and dedication as a passionate voice for your nonprofit. I wish you and your organization the very best as you work diligently to fulfill your mission.

If you'd like to reach out to me directly, please send me an email at maria@mariasatira.com, and I'd be honored to schedule a free 15-minute call with you.

Maria Satira

REFERENCES

AdeptPlus. (2021, June 10). *Nielsen DMA 2021 RANKINGS*. MediaTracks Communications. https://mediatracks.com/resources/nielsen-dma-rankings-2021/.

Federal Communications Commission. (2021, April 5). Broadcast Station Totals. Retrieved from https://docs.fcc.gov/public/attachments/DOC-371337A1.pdf

Gardner, A. B. (2016, August 14). Facebook. https://www.facebook.com/photo.php?fbid=10100531088756336.

Dietrich, G. (2020, September 7). *What is the peso model...and how do I use it?* Spin Sucks. https://spinsucks.com/communication/peso-model-breakdown/.

Karapetyan, A. (2016, November 26). Instagram. https://www.instagram.com/p/v2hjjND9S8.

Merriam-Webster. (n.d.). *Word*. Merriam-Webster. https://www.merriam-webster.com/dictionary/word.

News & Press. Food Bank of Central & Eastern North Carolina. (2021, April 15). https://foodbankcenc.org/.

Pew Research Center. (2020, January 9). *Pew Research Center*. Pew Research Center. https://www.pewresearch.org/.

U.S. Bureau of Labor Statistics. (2016, February 25). *Volunteering in the United States, 2015*. U.S. Bureau of Labor Statistics. https://www.bls.gov/news.release/volun.nr0.htm.

U.S. Bureau of Labor Statistics. (2018, August 31). *Nonprofits account for 12.3 million jobs, 10.2 percent of private-sector employment, in 2016*. U.S. Bureau of Labor Statistics. https://www.bls.gov/opub/ted/2018/nonprofits-account-for-12-3-million-jobs-10-2-percent-of-private-sector-employment-in-2016.htm.

ABOUT THE AUTHOR

Maria Satira is a multimedia and marketing professional with over a decade of experience in journalism, public relations, and corporate communications. She spent nearly 10 years as a news anchor and reporter in television markets along the East Coast – working for ABC, CBS, and CW affiliates. She later became the director of marketing and communications at an economic development organization and founded Maria Satira Media, LLC. This media relations and marketing consulting company focuses on assisting small businesses and not-for-profit organizations across the country achieve their digital marketing and communications goals.

Community involvement is of the utmost importance to Maria. She volunteers with various committees and boards to support local nonprofit organizations. She has served as a board member for various organizations, including the Humane Society of Eastern Carolina, Pitt County Arts Council at EMERGE, and Better Business Bureau Serving Eastern North Carolina. Maria is also a member of the advisory board for Riley's Army, Inc. and works with several marketing-based committees for organizations throughout eastern North Carolina.

Originally from Pittsburgh, Pennsylvania, Maria holds a Bachelor of Arts with majors in Media Arts and Communication from Robert Morris University. Through her involvement and support as an alumnus, she has been named to the university's prestigious President's Council.

Maria lives in Greenville with her husband, Andrew, and their two dogs, Badger and Yogi. The couple also owns and manages a property management company and a construction company that purchases, renovates, and rents properties in the downtown area. In addition to volunteering in their community, they enjoy traveling, spending time at the beach, and treasuring every moment with family and friends.